THEN
JESUS
CAME

The Gertrude Ticer Miracle

WINEPRESS WP PUBLISHING

ISBN 13: 978-1-57921-907-9
ISBN 10: 1-57921-907-1
Library of Congress Catalog Card Number: 2007924884

TABLE OF CONTENTS

FOREWORD

Thanks be to God that Gertrude Ticer's story is now in print for this generation and the generations to come. Jesus walked in to a hospital room. His touch brought an instantaneous healing to one who was blind, paralyzed, and already covered, deemed dead by the hospital staff. The knowledge of this mighty miracle, one of the greatest of the 20th century, has been saved in Gertrude's own anointed words. After transcribing Gertrude's testimony many years ago, Gail Lanier promised Gertrude that if no one else put her testimony of her healing into print, she would, and now we have it.

During the great outpouring of the Holy Spirit upon denominational churches in the 1960s and 70s, Gertrude came to Seattle. She stayed in our home several weeks. We had the privilege of taking her to give her testimony in churches, prayer groups, Full Gospel Business Men's meetings and Women's Aglow. Each time we heard it, God's awesome power and the depth of His love resonated in our hearts fresh and new.

As you read Gertrude's story, may your heart be filled with faith, the faith for your miracle. May her story be the beginning of a fresh outpouring of the Holy Spirit in all of our lives. Just as Gertrude learned, may we learn to turn away from the idolatries of this world and to turn our eyes upon Jesus, our first love. "With God all things are possible" (Mark 10:27).

Shade O'Driscoll and Fr. Dick O'Driscoll,
Associate Rector, (Ret)
St. Luke's Episcopal Church, Seattle, Washington

PREFACE

To the Readers of Gertrude Ticer's Story:

This book was compiled from audio tapes made of Gertrude sharing this miracle in various locations across the United States.

Retelling Gertrude's story was made possible with the help of those who deserve my heartfelt thanks. The magnitude of the task this amateur undertook was, no doubt, a direct incentive for your kind help. I appreciate that help and encouragement of those of you from Maryland to Florida, Virginia to Washington. Thank you for helping fulfill a promise made to Gertrude long ago.

Working with Gertrude's very own words has been a blessing I would wish for everyone. Take time to search out the wealth of riches hidden in this account. Gertrude had a walking, talking relationship with her Lord. May her story inspire you to begin or expand in depth and reality your own walk with God.

Gail Lanier

Gertrude Ticer

April 5, 1907 – April 8, 1982

"Jesus Christ the same yesterday,
today and forever."
Hebrews 13:8

INTRODUCTION

In 1962 my mother, Gertrude Ticer, was at the point of death in a Clark County hospital in Las Vegas, Nevada, when Jesus appeared to her! She was instantly healed, able to get out of bed, walk around, and tell everyone what had happened.

This began nearly two decades of being invited to share this experience in meetings. Even though she had been a shy person, not used to speaking in public, after this visit from Jesus she spoke with boldness everywhere. In one year she spoke from New York to Los Angeles, Canada to South America, and scores of places in between. She spoke in small home meetings and large auditoriums, small churches and large churches, sometimes speaking two times in a day.

There was no question that this event changed her life.

Randall Ticer,
Pastor,
Harvest Time Church, Lynnwood, Washington

PROLOGUE

**Trust in the LORD with all thine heart,
and lean not unto thine own understanding.
(Proverbs 3:5)**

You have had multiple sclerosis for years. There is no cure." When I heard my doctor say those words, I turned to God for my healing.

But, learning how to accept the healing I so earnestly desired was a long process as God patiently dealt with me through His Word. You needn't wait as long. I urge you to turn to God in the beginning.

I wasn't ready for a miracle at first. I agreed there was healing for other people, but I didn't realize I would not be healed by merely agreeing. Though I knew very little about healing, I could list the many qualifications I lacked. They all came under one heading—unbelief. I did not yet know I would have to believe.

For more than fifteen years I was the victim of multiple sclerosis, with its many crippling stages. At the end, I was completely paralyzed and totally blind.

On the road to my healing I had many struggles. I want to share with you what I experienced, both the good and the bad.

When I entered the hospital that last time it seemed the end was near. Yet, I still believed that God would heal me. I would not allow my faith to be shaken. As I lay under an oxygen tent during three separate heart attacks, I prayed. I was as certain then as I am now that faith is the gateway to communication with God. I believe anyone can say a silent prayer and when it reaches the Lord it will be loud.

> And it shall come to pass that, before they call,
> I will answer; and while they are yet speaking,
> I will hear.
>
> (Isaiah 65:24)

> Behold, the LORD's hand is not shortened, that
> it cannot save; neither his ear heavy, that it can-
> not hear.
>
> (Isaiah 59:1)

Before I learned to put Jesus first, I discovered I had to lay aside many things, including other gods, not loving my neighbor enough, and not forgiving fully.

Next, I asked God where I had limited Him. As He continued to bring Scripture to my memory, I realized I was keeping Him out of the present. At the end of my search, I received a much greater blessing from God than I could have imagined possible.

Do I believe in healing? I'm happy to say, yes, since I have been healed. I asked the Lord to heal me body, soul, and spirit. He heard my cry. He healed me spirit, soul, and body.

I asked God to send me someone to pray a prayer of faith and He did just that. Bea Schmick found me on July 1, 1962, and God healed me on July 4, 1962. Yes, Jesus came, He touched me, and He made me whole.

Gertrude Ticer

CHAPTER ONE

WOMAN, THERE'S NOTHING I CAN DO FOR YOU

**Therefore, turn thou to thy God.
(Hosea 12:6)**

On a ranch near Comanche, Texas, I was born on April 5, 1907. James Pate, my beloved father, was ranch foreman there where many of my childhood memories were formed. My parents, Christians in the Southern Baptist Church, took my brothers and me to Sunday school and church and raised us to be Christians. When I was seven, we moved to a farm in Ellis County, near Dallas.

During World War II, after I was grown and married, we moved to Las Vegas, Nevada, where my husband worked in a war plant in what is now nearby Henderson. After he entered the service and was later stationed in Germany, I continued to live in the desert, as always.

I thought I knew why I lived in Las Vegas. I believe now God has an ultimate purpose for everything we do. He placed me where He wanted me.

"Please tell me what's wrong with me," I asked my doctor. He was a friend of the family as well as our family physician, and I had every confidence in him. Due to a bad accident, I had many complications, making a diagnosis difficult for him. He had sent me to clinics in Phoenix, Beverly Hills, Los Angeles, and Fort Worth. I was finally insisting that he give me a diagnosis.

As I waited, it seemed as if he was reluctant to break the news to me.

Finally he said, "You have had multiple sclerosis for years. There is no cure."

My symptoms had come on gradually. First I began to stagger. Then I started to stumble and fall. Next I became color-blind and began seeing double. Later, my spine became paralyzed. The complications following the accident had caused symptoms that other MS patients might not experience.

"There was no need to tell you before," my doctor said. He began to explain the illness to me, assuring me he was already doing everything possible to help. He had started me on an individual treatment, typical protocol for MS patients, making it possible for me to be comfortable for long periods of time.

He told me that many similarities exist between multiple sclerosis and polio, with one main exception. Multiple sclerosis strikes over and over again, paralyzing more each time it strikes. The disease was once called "creeping paralysis." The name was changed, but it's still creeping.

That was when I turned to God and His Word. I began reading and studying about healing in the Bible. I shouldn't have waited so long. Doctors do wonderful things for their patients and medical science cures us of many things, but it is God who heals.

When some friends learned of the diagnosis, they asked me to see one more specialist in Las Vegas. Even though I was already seeking God for my healing, I agreed to go. He ran the usual tests for multiple sclerosis, including a spinal tap and taking some bone marrow. The specialist explained he would remove some tissue in an exploratory operation that would help him estimate how long I had had the disease. He also ordered an EKG, X-rays, and various nerve tests.

When the test results came back the specialist told me, "Woman, there's nothing I can do for you, nothing at all. You've had multiple sclerosis for more than fifteen years. According to these tests, complete paralysis and blindness are going to set in. Both should have happened before now."

Handing me a copy of the results he said, "I want you to go back to your clinic, but I'll make sure you are taken to an eye specialist and an eye bank tomorrow."

How I wanted an eye! When I went to the eye bank, I was told, much to my disappointment, I had come too late.

You can see in my sharing how I felt down deep inside that I didn't always do the right thing. I know God answered my prayers. I didn't get an eye, but He answered in the way that was best for me. After Jesus made me whole, I could see everyone and everything with my very own eyes.

Yes, the road to my healing was very long. We read in the Book of Daniel that his prayer was delayed. We are no different. God's timetable may be different from ours. We often don't even recognize the answer when it does come, but He will answer in the way best for us.   ■ ■ ■

CHAPTER TWO

I WANTED A LOGICAL ANSWER

**Ask thee for a sign of the Lord, thy God.
(Isaiah 7:11)**

The only way I could fly from Las Vegas to visit my family in Texas was to buy a wheelchair ticket. On one trip, a worker who loaded freight on the airplane walked by the counter and heard the clerk ask me, "How will we get you up into the plane?"

The good man stopped and said, "Why, I'll take you in that wheelchair up on the freight elevator and swing you right over to where the people sit." That was just one of the many acts of kindness I was shown through the years.

In Texas I stayed with my mother in Gatesville and the rest of my family came to visit. My precious mother was a widow, my father having been dead many years. My brother Casey also lived in Gatesville, and Glen in Fort Worth.

My third brother, Jack Pate, was at that time a minister in a community chapel in Dumas, Texas. During one of my visits Jack said, "Dear Sister, there's healing from God. I've laid hands on people and prayed and God healed them."

He then told me this story. "One Sunday morning a family brought a little boy to church with a badly bleeding foot. I rushed out of the pulpit and asked, 'Do you want me to call an ambulance?'

"'No, we brought him to church to be prayed for,' they replied.

"No one had ever asked me to do that before. I was scared. I stopped everything and stepped aside in the sanctuary. Leaning against a post I told the Lord, 'Oh, Lord, if You really want me to be this kind of pastor; if You really want me to pray for the sick to be healed, now is the time. If You want me in this kind of ministry, when I pray for that little boy You heal him!'

"I walked back to the boy, laid my hands on him and prayed. Quick as a flash, he turned and ran down the aisle and out the front door of the church. Leaving the rest behind, I ran after him. I was determined to catch him to find out what God had done.

"After running a block, I caught up with him and brought him back to the church. When the blood was washed off, it was apparent the boy's foot was completely healed."

My brother had his answer.

Years later when he related the story to me, he was still faithful to this call of God to pray for the sick. I knew he was telling me the truth, so I was happy to agree with him, but that didn't mean I believed I'd be healed.

At that time, I knew next to nothing about healing. I was in what you could call "the agreeing stage." Agreeing is not believing. It's even possible to agree out loud with people about many things, yet not believe a single word. I agreed and rejoiced others had been healed.

I had read about people being healed. But, it wasn't real, somehow, to read about someone I didn't know. They were "over there," I was "over here." I read the Bible, but I had never been to a healing service in my life and my church had never said a word to me about healing.

Perhaps I had heard there was a day or an age of healing long ago, I honestly don't know. I know now God is as willing to heal today as when He healed people 2,000 years ago.

But, I didn't understand this then. My brother's words landed on poor soil. They settled right in the middle of my logic where there was no room for a supernatural act of God.

As a result, I was as crippled flying back to Las Vegas as I was when I flew down to Texas.

■ ■ ■

CHAPTER THREE

EVEN ME, LORD, EVEN ME?

God is no respecter of persons.
(Acts 10:34)

If you need healing, or you have a loved one who needs it, healing is important to you. But, it's more difficult to pray and believe for yourself than for your neighbor. If you're "down" in a wheelchair, and you want to be "up" out of it, it is not easy to bring that healing to yourself.

Your only foundation is the Word of God. In fact, it is your protection against many things. The Word says God does the healing, and He would just as soon do it today as He did 2,000 years ago. My church didn't teach healing, but my Bible did.

> He sent his word, and healed them, and
> delivered them from their destructions.
> (Psalm 107:20)

One question I asked the Lord over and over was, "Who is healing for?" He answered by bringing to my memory a verse I knew from the Word of God.

> . . . for I am the LORD that healeth thee.
> (Exodus 15:26)

Peter asked, "Where else shall we turn?" Even though I knew very little about healing, I knew enough to turn to God according to His promises in the Word. Sometimes it depends on how badly we need God's help and His Word, before we turn to Him. I needed Him and I wanted to be delivered from my destruction.

> I perceive that God is no respecter of persons.
> (Acts 10:34)

"Even me, Lord? Even me?" I asked. If healing had been given on merits, He surely would have passed me by. I had not one single merit for Him to heal even one sore little toe, let alone multiple sclerosis!

The seed my brother planted long before finally took root. I was now in the "believing stage." There was much I didn't understand, but that did not stop me from believing God's Word.

Not knowing how to accept healing was one way I limited God. I didn't know I had to do something. I waited for Him to strike me, maybe like lightning, and make me whole. But, that didn't happen. I had to do something. I had to learn to reach out by faith and accept healing for myself. You can see I needed much help from the Lord.

After I was healed, a doctor asked me, "Why didn't this happen fifteen years ago?"

"I believe I wasn't ready," I told him.

God has an appointed time. That time is now. Have the requirements been met? You say, "That's easy."

No, it is not easy. Among other things, you must believe. The Greek word believe means to adhere to, trust in, and rely on the Lord.

> LORD, I believe; help thou mine unbelief.
>
> (Mark 9:24)

When I said, "Now, Lord, I don't have any unbelief," He showed me my unbelief. I quickly changed my prayer to, "Lord, just help my unbelief."

Even for salvation, the greatest miracle of all, a condition must be met. He will not, He cannot, go against your will.

> For God so loved the world, that he gave his only begotten Son, that whosoever believeth in him should not perish, but have everlasting life.
>
> (John 3:16)

I do not believe God makes us sick. If He did, we couldn't ask Him to turn around and heal us. He will not play on both sides of the fence. God is our Healer. He does not make us sick.

■ ■ ■

CHAPTER FOUR

MY KEY

**Jesus Christ, the same yesterday,
and today and forever.
(Hebrews 13:8)**

It came alive to me that Jesus Christ is the same yesterday, and today, and forever. When I truly believed this, God gave me this as my *key* Scripture. It seemed to jump right up out of the page at me. It was plainer than any other Scripture to me. I knew for certain it was mine to use. With this verse He enabled me to unlock many healing Scriptures I had read but never applied to myself.

God let me know He would still do today the miracles He performed as recorded in the Gospels and throughout all the Word. Nothing is impossible for God. The Bible says Jesus is the same; Jesus is the answer; Jesus is the key to whatever we need.

. . . with his stripes we are healed.

(Isaiah 53:5)

This promise is for "whosoever will"—whosoever will believe, whosoever will meet the requirements. I still didn't understand it all, but I kept on believing God would heal me according to His Word.

As I continued to ponder Isaiah 53:5, I realized Isaiah the prophet was looking toward the time when the Messiah would come and would bear those thirty-nine stripes on His back. Peter, looking back at Calvary, said:

> . . . by whose stripes ye were healed.
>
> (1 Peter 2:24)

When I read those words I saw that Peter used the past tense when he said, "ye *were* healed" (emphasis added). I told the Lord, "Then, I *was* healed before I was. Those stripes laid on Your back at Calvary were for my healing even before I came to be."

> He himself took our infirmities, and bore our sicknesses.
>
> (Matthew 8:17)

These Scriptures revealed to me healing is included in the Atonement. The Atonement was when Jesus Christ died for my sins and shed His blood for the remission of my sins. The Scriptures declare He suffered those thirty-nine stripes on His back for your healing and mine. God did His part at Calvary. Not only was it for my spirit and my soul, healing was for my body.

■ ■ ■

CHAPTER FIVE

WHEN GOD
HEALS ME

**Having, therefore, these promises.
(2 Corinthians 7:1)**

"Mother, I'll buy you a good wheelchair so you won't be so handicapped," my son Randy told me while I was visiting him in California.

"Randy, I don't believe there is such a thing as a good wheelchair. When God heals me, what will I do with it?"

"Oh, you can give it to someone else."

"I wouldn't want to give a wheelchair to someone. I'd rather say, 'God can heal you, too.'"

I had begun to pray:

> Heal me, O LORD, and I shall be healed.
> (Jer. 17:14)

I was not a good patient. Thinking I was over the attacks, I would get out of the wheelchair, holding on to the back, because I couldn't get my feet off the floor. One day I fell over a hot stove. It took some time before I could raise myself up to get off. That day I wished I had stayed in my wheelchair.

"What are you trying to prove by trying to get out of your wheelchair?" my doctor asked me.

"I believe the Lord is going to heal me. I thought I was defeating myself by depending on the wheelchair," I told him.

"I'll not tell you to go back and sit in that wheelchair all the time, but I will tell you to never cook another meal. Just stay away from a hot stove."

Having therefore these promises . . .

(2 Cor. 7:1)

A gentleman from the Veterans of Foreign Wars came to my home and asked, "Do you believe God is going to heal you?"

"I certainly do."

"If you really believe that, then we'll loan you walkers, wheelchairs, lifters. We'll loan you any equipment you need while you're paralyzed." They kept their word, bringing items to my home and picking them up when I no longer needed them. The people at the Veterans of Foreign Wars in Las Vegas were happy when God healed me.

Even though the paralysis became more severe, I remembered these words:

. . . and they were healed everyone.

(Acts 5:16)

I continued to say, "*When* God heals me . . ." never *if.* I made plans for when it would happen.

"When the Lord heals me, I'll take you to Disneyland," I told my grandson Tom one day.

He looked at me and asked, "Do you really believe the Lord's going to make you well?"

"Yes."

"Then why are you still sitting in that wheel chair?" That is one of the most insightful questions anyone ever asked me.

> . . . behold, now is the day of salvation.
>
> (2 Corinthians 6:2)

If *now* is the appointed time for salvation, *now* is the appointed time for healing because of what Christ did for us in the Atonement.

I learned that:

> God hath dealt to every man *the* measure of faith.
>
> (Romans 12:3)

I wondered if He would use a big measure or a small measure with me until I learned it was "the measure of faith."

> Looking unto Jesus, the author and finisher of our faith;
>
> (Hebrews 12:2)

Be sure to build on that measure with the Word of God. Have faith and know where it comes from. Do you look to the Author? And then do you go to the Finisher?

> So, then, faith cometh by hearing, and hearing by the word of God.
>
> (Romans 10:17)

How did I get healed? By the grace of God through faith—grace, that unmerited favor of God.

■ ■ ■

CHAPTER SIX

JUST INSIDE THE DOOR

After that the Holy Ghost is come upon you.
(Acts 1:8)

Aneighbor not only had experienced the Baptism in the Holy Spirit, she lived it day by day. I wanted the Lord to baptize me in the Holy Spirit, but I didn't understand speaking in tongues. It scared me. I spent three nights at church before I received this wonderful gift. (When I buy a pair of shoes, I always take the tongues along with the shoes.)

After receiving the Baptism in the Holy Spirit, I had a wonderful new prayer life. I prayed in a way I had never prayed before. The Holy Spirit quickened my spirit and opened the Word to me, helping me study the Word better. I saw the Word, and myself, in a new way.

There is a Holy Spirit faith. You can have a faith that, simply put, isn't much. But, you can have a faith inspired by the Holy Spirit, fueled by the Baptism in the Holy Spirit that builds you up.

I couldn't count the times I had read the Bible before. But, prayerfully studying the Word is the only way to healing and the only way for a closer walk with God. I found it a wonderful thing as I began to pray over the Word of God, asking God to open my understanding and quicken my spirit to understand it in depth.

The Word of God is our only foundation, not what someone, even someone in authority, says it is. If you're not sure, search it to find out for yourself. We may have every experience in the Word that is approved by God, but we don't want any experience that does not agree with the Word. If it is of God, it will be found there and will not, in any way, be contrary. If it's in the Word, if it's scriptural, it's for you and you may receive it.

My son, Randy, now an ordained minister, says, "If God meant for us to have more, God would have put that in the Word, too."

The Holy Spirit will inspire us to rightly divide God's precious Word. God help us to not omit something or use it carelessly. You are authorized by Jesus Christ Himself to give God's Word to others. He does not want that authority neglected.

When I received salvation I wanted the Lord to let everyone stay there with me. When I received the Baptism in the Holy Spirit, I thought I'd like to stay there. When I received healing, I thought, "This is a good place, Lord. I'll stay here."

But, we never stay in any one place. Unless we're going forward, we're going backward. Unless we push uphill, we slide downhill. I realized the day I received the Baptism in the Holy Spirit was a brand new day.

The answer of the tongue is from the LORD.
(Proverbs 16:1)

Did you ever hear the phrase, "pray through?" I was taken to a church where I heard only those two words from the sermon and took them home with me. I had never heard pray through mentioned from the pulpit before. I didn't understand what the words meant. I didn't yet know what it was I would go through. I didn't know what my destination would be when I got there. The preacher planted a seed that night, but it was planted in a prideful heart. The seed, once again, lodged in my logic. I wanted a logical explanation for the reason to pray through.

But I prayed through—in my wheelchair. I found I was praying through my inhibitions, other people's ideas, through what others had said. When I reached the destination, I knew I was in the presence of God. It was wonderful to pray myself and have the prayers of my family, but I learned to pray until I knew I was in the presence of the One who heard and answered my prayers. It didn't take me long to do that again! After I had prayed through I truly believed God would heal me, but I didn't know how it would happen.

Praying through has great value. I heard someone say, "That was years ago when they prayed through." It may not please others, but it still pleases the Lord. That was the way I began to exercise my faith. I believe He waits to be acknowledged.

Are you paralyzed in your spirit? You can pray through that. You can pray through anything holding you back. Whatever you need, you can pray through until you truly know you are in the presence of God, the One who has the answer. ■ ■ ■

CHAPTER SEVEN

AFTER ALL, I WAS A CHRISTIAN

Love thy neighbor as thyself.
(Leviticus 19:18)

I was sure I was right with God. After all, I had been a Christian in the Southern Baptist Church for twenty-five years.

Then the Lord asked me through the Word, "Do you love your neighbor as yourself?"

I had to answer, "No, no, Lord. Some I don't even like!" Again, it was time for, "Forgive me, Lord; forgive me."

Forgiving others was involved, too. I had to forgive others. Then again it was, "Forgive me."

I learned it's not how much I said to others, but how much I loved them. That's after they sinned against me and I forgave them. Did I love them as much as before it happened? I didn't and I found that I hadn't experienced forgiveness. You can see this Christian was breaking some of God's Ten Commandments.

It was as though I heard, "If Jesus abides in you and you abide in Him, you'll love your neighbor with the love of Jesus." He had weighed me in the balance again and found me wanting.

Ask, and it shall be given you.

(Matthew 7:7)

Have you ever known anyone who asked God for healing on her own terms? Look no further. I would say a short little prayer, then give Him a long answer. I'd tell Him and tell Him, and the Word says to ask.

"Now, Lord, heal me because I'm an accountant and the people at the college promised me a job when You heal me," I'd pray.

I even told God, "I'll give 20 percent, even 50 percent, to Your work," proving how little I knew about the requirements for healing.

What I said came between Jesus and me. How foolish I must have sounded in the ears of my Lord!

I shouldn't have turned around and given the Lord the answer after I prayed. I was laying down the answer, not with words, but with my attitude. My attitude said, "Lord, heal me—on my terms. Lord, make me whole—on my terms." I wanted to live my life out my way.

I made excuses for my unbelief, for my false pride. When those excuses weren't good enough, I made promises to God I couldn't keep. Can you keep your vows to God? I couldn't because I wasn't fully trusting Him. I learned making vows to God is a serious thing.

In the midst of all the promises I couldn't keep, I remembered, "all the silver and all the gold and all the cattle on a thousand hills belong to God." He didn't need me, I needed Him. My promises to Him were of no value. My healing would never happen that way. Jesus is the Master. When I realized that, it was much easier to turn it all over to Him, to trust Him in my heart, and learn to ask Him to heal me on His terms.

■ ■ ■

CHAPTER EIGHT

BOYS, YOU'VE FORGOTTEN SOMETHING

And your feet shod with the preparation of the Gospel of peace.
(Ephesians 6:15)

One morning my doctor said, "You should have someone with you at all times."

That evening at 7:00 o'clock I became completely paralyzed. The ambulance I had been in many times before arrived to take me to the hospital. Both attendants, young enough to be my sons, knew me by name. They thought I would be panicky, but I said, "No, I'm not panicky. I have Jesus."

As they carried me out to the ambulance, I said, "Boys, you've forgotten something."

"What did we forget?"

"You didn't bring my shoes." I had my Bible, I had my gown and robe on, but I was missing my pair of shoes. I had carefully planned ahead. I reasoned my feet would be tender, having not been walked on for so long. I would need shoes when God healed me.

In the back of the ambulance, the intern who was giving me oxygen said, "Now, Gertrude, you know you're paralyzed. We tried to straighten you out on this stretcher, but we had to leave you just the way you are. Now, tell me, what would a paralyzed woman do with a pair of shoes?"

"One day the Lord's going to make me whole again, and I'll need them when I walk out of the hospital."

    . . . your shoes on your feet.

            (Exodus 12:11)

At the hospital I continued to pester people for my shoes until a nurse's aide agreed to go to my apartment for them. When she returned she said, "I couldn't bring you any shoes. All of your things have been packed up and moved out so someone else could have your apartment."

"Oh, what did they do with my clothes?"

"I don't know, neither do your neighbors." She looked at me and said, "You know, more than once I've seen the doctor try to get some kind of a reaction in your feet, but he never did."

"No, it felt like he was sticking the pin in the bedspread. I felt nothing."

"Now, what would you do with a pair of shoes?"

"When the Lord makes me whole it won't be easy to walk barefoot."

Later, I had some visitors who said, "We know you like 7-Up, but we can't give you any for fear you might choke. We would bring you some food, but it has to be weighed and measured. There's just nothing we can bring you."

"Oh, yes there is. You can buy me a pair of shoes."

My visitors didn't mind buying the shoes, but it was another thing to be seen bringing them into an incurable ward for someone completely paralyzed and blind. It was clear they did not believe someone in my condition would ever walk out of an incurable ward.

I must have sounded like a parrot! I'd say, "One day the Lord's going to heal me. Please leave my Bible here, my shoes there, and please leave one robe. Don't throw away my duster."

"But, Gertrude, you're paralyzed," they'd say. "You won't need your duster."

"You can't see to read your Bible—you're blind."

"We can't get shoes on your crippled, twisted feet."

They must have gotten tired of trying to explain it to me.

Yet I believed. Nothing could alter that fact.

■ ■ ■

CHAPTER NINE

DOING THINGS MY WAY

So foolish was I.
(Psalm 73:22)

It was late spring when I remembered a fenced-in yard with a tree that would be in full leaf. I asked to be taken outside to breathe some of that fresh air again and get away from the stale hospital smells. I wearied people with this until the charge nurse came to my bed and helped me understand what I wanted was impossible.

"Ticer, don't you know there's no way we can take you outside unless we find enough orderlies to carry you outside in your bed? We simply can't move you any other way now because of your condition. Can't you understand this?"

"Yes, I see that now. I apologize."

I had to learn to trust Jesus.

> Trust in the LORD with all thine heart, and lean
> not unto thine own understanding.
> (Proverbs 3:5)

Knowing the Word said this and doing it myself were two different things. Remember, I'm sharing with you both the good and the bad about myself. Many times I thought I was trusting the Lord, but I still held back just a little. Doing things my way was different from what the Word said. How easy it is to step out of God's will!

I had to learn to lay things down at the feet of Jesus, at an altar, or on the altar of my heart. I like to think I laid them on the altar of my heart. He knew I would take back what I'd given Him. Not only did I have to learn to trust Him, I had to learn to trust Him *completely*.

> What doth the LORD require of thee?
>
> (Micah 6:8)

It was easier to meet the requirements for my healing, for my miracle, than it was to meet the requirements for the purpose of that miracle. I began to understand that God heals for a purpose. I needed to be able to meet the requirements for the purpose. I needed to seriously think about that.

The Lord let me know there would be an act of obedience— what was called at one time an act of sacrifice. He said in a still, small voice to me, "Yield your spirit to God. Submit your will to God daily."

When I began to submit my will to God, I found I had a cross of my own.

> . . . come, take up the cross, and follow me.
>
> (Mark 10:21)

I learned the word would be "go." I had some dear little ones. I didn't want to leave those precious little arms my grand-children so often slipped around my neck.

I couldn't get away from this cross. I couldn't erase it and the Lord didn't move it. I had to be willing to do this act of obedience. As I took up my cross, I found Jesus made it lighter the closer I walked with Him.

> Submit yourselves, therefore, to God.
>
> (James 4:7)

The Lord said for me to submit my will to Him daily. I had to rid myself of strong self-will to start becoming an empty vessel. That was hard for me. We all have it. It is strong in everyone. Even babies use it to get their own way.

I found I could submit my will for a little while, maybe fifteen minutes, or an hour, sometimes two. It was one thing to get in the will of God, but it was another to stay there, especially as I was in such need and asking for something from God. No one needed to throw me a stumbling block—I stumbled all over my self. I found I couldn't stay in His will because my mind would wander to my other gods—the things I looked to besides Him.

I discovered I had been submitting my will daily to the circumstances in my life, which is the easy way. Not only daily, I was submitting my will to my circumstances minute by minute. We yield our spirit to God once and for all. But, to stay in His will daily, we are to submit our will to the Lord, not to our circumstances.

> But seek ye first the kingdom of God, and his righteousness.
>
> (Matthew 6:33)

Have you yielded your spirit to God? Do you submit your will to Him every day? Maybe you know the first part of Matthew 6:33, but do you submit your will to God before you seek? If so, you'll know you're in the will of God when you do find.

The second part, seeking His righteousness, is too often forgotten. If you look in the Word, it plainly tells us there is only the righteousness of God. Self-righteousness, in His eyes, is as filthy rags.

> And all our righteousnesses are as filthy rags;
>
> (Isaiah 64:6)

45

As I began emptying out my old self-will, I remembered, God bless her, my dear mother saying, "God helps those who help themselves." But, in my case, I was at the end of my rope. So I laid everything on the altar before God. He began to help me when I said, "Lord, I can't do any more with this life. You take it." That's when He took over, as I laid on that bed, blind and paralyzed.

■ ■ ■

CHAPTER TEN

ONLY ONE REASON, NOW

**The desire accomplished is sweet to the soul.
(Proverbs 13:19)**

Don't waste any breath, Ticer, you've had another heart attack," the nurse told me. "It's my duty to keep you quiet." A special nurse was assigned to me around the clock during my heart attacks.

But, I could pray under that oxygen tent—oh, I could pray. I prayed until I knew God answered. Even a silent prayer, when it reaches the Lord, will be loud.

> And it shall come to pass that, before they call,
> I will answer; and while they are yet speaking,
> I will hear.
>
> (Isaiah 65:24)

After pondering "before they call, I will answer," I realized God recorded that in the Word to tell us He knew our very thoughts. That's how He answers before you call. That's how you can pray a silent prayer and know He hears you.

The day came when I was able to pray, "Lord, I believe in healing, and I don't want to die. I have only one reason now for wanting to live. Neither of my two children is as close to You as I wish they were. Let me go back and speak the Word of God to them."

There are times when reasons drop away quickly. I thought maybe I had taught my children my convictions. I realized I could have my own opinions, but teaching them to my children was not to be.

"Please turn me on my side so I can be facing my home," I asked. My home had been down at the very end of Charleston Street, on the edge of the desert. At times, they would turn me, having wrapped me in a sheet a certain way that kept me from rolling onto my back. I had some comfort thinking about my home and my children, those I loved and cared about. Or, I would think of the time before I was completely blind and paralyzed, when I was only crippled with multiple sclerosis.

Thou shalt have no other gods before me.
(Exodus 20:3)

Wanting to be pointed in that one direction showed I was dwelling on those I loved all too well. Other gods can slip in so easily and I discovered some of mine. "Forgive me, Lord, forgive me. I've been worshipping my children."

I expected healing any minute, yet I still lacked many qualifications. I could love my children, of course, but I had gone beyond just loving them. I had been dwelling on them and I had to put my priorities in the right order.

Lo, I am with you always.
(Matthew 28:20)

There were times when I even cried for my mother. When you're ill, maybe *you* don't cry for your mother, but I did. I'd say, "If only my family could be here," knowing that was impossible. Every time I cried out for my loved ones, He let me know, "I'm here; I'm here."

As I lay on my bed I remembered the words Jesus asked the paralyzed man at the Pool of Bethesda:

Wilt thou be made whole?

(John 5:6)

"Yes, Lord," I answered Him. "I'll be made whole. While You're at it, please don't just make me better, Lord. Reach down and make me whole again. They will put me back in another wheelchair, and I've already had a wheelchair experience. I don't want to go back to that."

God heard this cry. But, still I lay there, paralyzed and blind.

Jesus is saying to you, "Wilt thou be made whole?" You may not have multiple sclerosis or some other crippling condition. God will meet your every need. You can pray and God will hear you and answer your cry.

■ ■ ■

CHAPTER ELEVEN

WALKING, WITH SHOES ON

**How beautiful are thy feet with shoes,
O prince's daughter!
(The Song of Solomon 7:1)**

I did not become totally blind until those last few weeks in the hospital, but my mind remained clear the entire time. Shortly after I lost the last bit of my sight, Mr. Martin, a registered nurse and pre-med student in charge of our ward eight hours a day, came to my bed. He touched me on the head and said, "You've always been all right up here, Ticer, but someone's going to begin to wonder about you."

"Oh, tell me why." I was still full of self-pride.

"Because you have a Bible over here that you can't read, and a pair of shoes over there you can't wear."

"Let me tell you about my Bible and my shoes. I remember many of the healing Scriptures. These I believe. I remember many of the Psalms of David. They're going to console me while I'm here. I remember many of the promises of God. God grant that I may step from one promise to another when I walk out of your hospital. And I know Jesus Christ is the same yesterday, today, and forever."

Mr. Martin's footsteps echoed as he walked away without saying another word.

I believe it was God who gave me a faith vision of myself walking, with shoes on. God knew what I had been given, what I believed, and when I believed it. I had faith, I knew from whence it came, and I continued to build it by the Word of God.

Not long after that a young doctor walked to my bedside and said, "I'd like to know how you see yourself."

"Doctor, do you want just a nice reply? Do you really want an answer, or did you just come to talk?"

"No, I want an answer."

"Doctor, I don't see myself lying here as anything less than a human being." Thinking I couldn't hear, some of the staff would often remark about my condition as they pulled the curtains around my bed when others in the ward had visitors.

"How do you see yourself?"

"Walking! Walking, with shoes on!"

I believed. I knew not how to "unbelieve."

■ ■ ■

CHAPTER TWELVE

"I" ISN'T IN GOD'S ALPHABET

**Within myself I can do nothing.
(Philippians 4:13)**

My list of reasons for wanting to live was becoming smaller until I had narrowed it down to just a few. But, a spoon defeated me. When neither a heart attack nor a stroke put me down, a spoon did. At mealtimes I would think, "Oh, here comes that spoon again." I didn't have to have sight to know when it was coming. I could think clearly, but I wasn't able to get my thinking down to the movement that was to follow the thought. It was difficult for my body to follow a command from my brain.

They would give me a bite, but I wasn't ready to chew. When I began to think "chew," I wasn't chewing. They'd give me another bite, but I hadn't chewed the first bite yet. Before I knew it, another bite was there. I was supposed to swallow, but I hadn't even started chewing.

I couldn't speak loud enough to make anyone hear what I said. I wasn't able to shout. I couldn't get in any special position because I was paralyzed. But, there was one thing I could do.

I could pray. I prayed until I was on speaking terms with the Lord. He heard me and I knew when my prayers had been answered.

I still had something special to be thankful for. I believed Jesus was with me, and it didn't matter to Him how I appeared on the outside.

Because He was looking down on my heart and soul, I cried out, "Show me myself just the way You see me." I even cried out loud so He would show me how He saw me on the inside, not the way I saw myself, or the way others saw me.

He began to show me and I didn't like what I saw. All I could see was the capital letter "I" and "I" is not found in God's alphabet.

■ ■ ■

CHAPTER THIRTEEN

THE CROSS IS EMPTY

**He came, therefore, and took the body of Jesus.
(John 19:38)**

You may think it strange, but I found benefits in being blind. I could no longer see what people were doing "over here," or what was happening "over there." No longer did men or things distract or hinder me. Now, I could see the Cross. My physical sight had given way to my spiritual sight. My only hindrance was the footsteps I had to take, because now I could walk only by faith. Seeing them for the first time, I could have said, "Lord, my feet won't fit," but Jesus made sure they fit perfectly.

I learned the Lord Jesus Christ wanted to lead me back to the foot of the Cross so I would know my Jesus had truly been resurrected from the dead. He was no longer hanging on that Cross. He was still saying, through the Word, that He was the same today as He was yesterday and will be forever.

Only at the foot of that empty Cross, where Jesus met me, have I found the ground level. Nowhere else has that been the case.

As I started getting forgiveness and more forgiveness, giving forgiveness and more forgiveness, I was able to begin putting Jesus first. It was not easy for me. It took time.

The day did come when I was able to say, "Lord, those I love so well are at my back forevermore, and I've put this life of mine there, too." I had put all that pain behind me. I could not dwell on it every minute and still have Jesus first. I was able to put Jesus between the pain and me. Instead, I would think about the wonders of Jesus.

"Lord, make me whole, spirit, soul and body," I'd pray. Then I'd ask, "What will You have me do?" He knew whether I meant tonight, tomorrow, or if I meant forevermore.

When I spoke those words, I knew one thing, I was close to Jesus. I found He could communicate many things to me with no speech or sound. He continued to bring what I had read and studied in the Word of God to my memory. I had rid myself of things that were between Jesus and me.

But, I was still in bed, paralyzed and blind. So, I knew I was continuing to limit God in some way.

My heart was no longer turned toward where I had lived or what was before. I prayed, "Lord, I'm like Hezekiah. I've turned my face to the wall. It's only Father, Son, and Holy Spirit here with me now. I've put You first. I've prayed a prayer of faith, but I'm still paralyzed and I'm still blind. How have I put the limits on You, Lord?"

He brought to my memory Moses stepping aside to see why the bush wasn't consumed as it continued to burn (Exodus 3:3). God reminded me that we, too, are to step aside to see what God is doing or what He wants us to do.

Then God brought three other Scriptures to my memory. Moses, bringing the children of Israel out of Egypt, asked God what he should say to the people when they would ask the name of the God of their fathers:

> And God said unto Moses, I AM THAT I AM:
> (Exodus 3:14)

Jesus Christ said, I am the Way, the Truth and
the Life;

(John 14:6)

Now faith is . . .

(Hebrews 11:1)

Lying paralyzed on my bed thinking about those Scriptures,
I began to understand. When I talked about what Jesus had
done in the Gospels and on the shores of Galilee I was talking
about the past. When I said, "One day the Lord will make
me whole," I was talking about the future. Never had I said
"today." He wanted me to know "I am that I am" and "faith is"
are in the present tense. They are in my *now*!

■ ■ ■

CHAPTER FOURTEEN

VISITS WITH
MR. PHILLIPS

Let them give glory unto the LORD.
(Isaiah 42:12)

Mr. Phillips would come over to say hello and visit with me when he came to see his wife's grandmother in the same ward. He was a civil engineer and a prominent, well-educated gentleman who was working on a short-term project in Las Vegas.

It wasn't my usual habit to speak with people about their souls or about the Bible, but I did with Mr. Phillips. I even gave him Scriptures to read.

One time he said, "I enjoy these talks about the Bible. When you go home, I won't have anyone else to visit with besides Grandmother." Then he asked me, "When are you going home?"

My physical deterioration was not yet too noticeable. The head of my bed was elevated to prevent my head from falling various ways. The sheet was tucked up under my neck hiding my paralyzed body.

"I'm not going home right now," I said.

Mr. Phillips and I had two different places in mind. He was referring to my apartment. I believed Jesus would heal me. Going home to Heaven was a long way off for me.

He stopped at the desk after this conversation to ask when I would be dismissed from the hospital.

"She's not going anywhere," the nurse said.

The next time he came, he asked about my condition.

"I have multiple sclerosis," I answered. "Under this sheet I'm paralyzed. I can do nothing."

We continued to visit and talk about various Scriptures every time he came.

After my condition worsened, I was moved out of that ward into another where the only visitors allowed were family. One day he came into the new ward through the adjoining bathroom and found me. I was blind by then and my physical appearance had changed drastically.

Standing by my bed, he said, "I want you to know I am back with the Lord. I received forgiveness and I'm walking closer to Jesus than ever before. If it hadn't been for you I never would have come back to God." I could feel his tears on my hand as he held it.

"Why me?" I asked. "You could have gone to any minister, any theologian, and he would have told you how or helped you get back to the Lord."

"I would not have gone to any of them. I would never have listened. But, I found a paralyzed patient who spoke to me about the Lord. Out of that misery, someone was concerned about my soul! I got on my knees and I prayed to God again. I never would have done it otherwise, never."

Mr. Phillips brought his wife and two children to see me after that, again through the connecting bathroom. As they stood by my bed, his wife said, "I wish we could do something for you."

I said, "Let's give the glory to God; let's give our praise to Jesus. You two go walk with the Lord and serve Jesus. You have God's blessings from me."

■ ■ ■

CHAPTER FIFTEEN

I SENT THIS WOMAN TO YOU

**Is not this the fast that I have chosen?
(Isaiah 58:6)**

L ord, there is something I still don't know," I prayed one day. "Please send me somebody who will pray a prayer of faith." He sent someone, but not immediately.

Then Bea Schmick came. I knew she was small because I could feel her breath on my face as she spoke. I learned later she was younger than my daughter.

She stood by my bed and asked, "Do you believe God can heal you?" That was a safe question for the timid person that she was.

"Yes."

"Do you want me to pray?"

"Yes."

She said a simple little prayer and walked away.

I didn't know she was the one God had sent. So many times we miss those God sends to us.

"I sent this woman to you."

That was the first time in my life I ever heard Jesus speak. I didn't even know it was possible. If I had known, I would have asked to hear Him long before then. I can't say it was the first time He ever spoke to me, but it was the first time I ever heard Him. I had never been so close to Him before.

But Bea Schmick was gone. I was blind, so I couldn't describe her. I didn't remember her name. My bed was in the corner of the room. I had no bells to ring, no buttons to push. I couldn't have used them even if I had seen them. After much effort, I was able to get Bea back to my bedside.

I told her, "The Lord said, 'I sent this woman to you.'"

"Yes," she said. "In Baltimore, the Lord told me to go to an incurable ward in a hospital in Las Vegas, Nevada. I was to pray for the one who said those very words."

We wept and we cried and we prayed together.

I praise God there are people who can hear and will obey the Lord's voice today. Bea and Smitty, her husband, came from Baltimore, Maryland, and had a temporary home in Las Vegas. Bea had been in every other hospital in the city but the one I was in. She found me on July 1, 1962.

After she visited me she went home and began a strict fast, without food and without water for three days. I had heard of fasts without food, but not without water. Three days and three nights of going without food and water in the hot July desert was not easy.

Every evening Bea came back to the hospital to pray. Her prayers at the hospital were short. She saved her long prayers for home. I wonder, in the eyes of God, if Bea Schmick is special to Him.

Those next three days my condition worsened. I had prayed for the Lord to not just make me better, but to make me whole. I felt disappointed, yet, everything was going according to God's plan. He meant this to be a miracle, not a healing.

I am thankful that there was someone in Baltimore who knew how to fast and pray and would perform an act of obedience.

God spoke to Bea; that was all she needed. Smitty only had what Bea said God told her. It was easy for Bea. It was hard for Smitty. "Thank you, Bea," and "Thank you, thank you, Smitty."

■ ■ ■

CHAPTER SIXTEEN

FUNERAL ARRANGEMENTS

**An evil disease, say they, cleaveth fast upon him.
(Psalm 41:8)**

On July 3, I felt a sheet being laid over me and the sides tucked in. As an MS patient, I experienced a lag between thinking and moving. As soon as I could, I moved the one elbow that still had a bit of mobility in it. The nurse removed the sheet and sent for a doctor. After making another spinal tap, the doctor said, "Send for someone to make funeral arrangements."

Tom, my young grandson, who lived nearby, was called and asked to come to the hospital. The results of the spinal tap were explained to him, and he was told to begin making funeral arrangements.

On the morning of July 4, my mother, children, and brothers were called.

At twilight on July 4, 1962, Bea came to my bed and asked, "Do you believe God will heal you? Do you really believe He will?" This time she said "will," not "can."

"Yes."

"Even now?"

"Even now."

"Do you know unless you're healed tonight there's no more time?"

"I know."

To me, no more time meant something far different than what it meant to those in the hospital. They thought I was in a coma and not able to hear, but I heard every word. In spite of what they said, I still believed God would heal me. Nothing altered that.

No more time meant He would heal me now. Down deep inside I was praising God, because that meant no more waiting time. What a joyful moment for me!

Bea asked me, "If I bring a glass of ice water and set it here by your bed, do you believe you could swallow all that water and not be as thirsty as you are right now? Do you believe that?"

"Oh, yes!" That was easy to believe because my liquids were limited and I was thirsty all the time.

"But if I bring it here and set it down on this table by your bed and you don't pick it up and you don't drink a drop of it, would you be just as thirsty as you are right now?"

"Yes."

When Bea mentioned water, I knew why the Lord had sent her all the way from Baltimore. I knew God sent Bea to me. She had been without water herself for the past three days of her fast in the hot July of the desert. Bea could identify with the constant thirst I experienced.

She asked me, "Did you accept Jesus Christ as your Savior?"

"Yes."

"Have you accepted the Baptism in the Holy Spirit?"

"Yes."

"Accept healing. They're all gifts. God sent me here to teach you acceptance. How did you receive Jesus Christ as your personal Savior?"

"By faith."

"Reach out by faith and accept healing. You believe in healing, now accept it. It was paid for at Calvary by the thirty-nine stripes put on Jesus' back. It is here."

Bea said acceptance is truly believing God's healing power is here for all. If someone extends a gift to me, either I reach out and accept it, or I refuse it. It won't do me any good if I don't take it. I had to accept healing for myself.

> Is any among you afflicted, let him pray.
>
> (James 5:13)

She said, "You must pray for yourself. I'm going to pray for you again, but you must pray, too."

After she prayed, she said, "Raise your hands and pray."

I was trying with all of my heart. Wouldn't you raise your hands for a gift from your Heavenly Father? He knew if I could, I would have raised my hands.

Bea later told me one finger on one hand moved.

Again, she said, "Pray."

"Lord, I believe, I believe. I will accept this healing for myself and now, Lord."

It was then I heard Jesus say in that beautiful voice, "Go and say, 'God healed me.' Go to the people who believe in healing and to the people who don't believe. Go to the people who will laugh and the people who will scorn, and then testify."

The Lord already had me get rid of any thought of independence. Neither was there room for any of the little, insignificant words I might substitute for hate or dislike. He had shown me there was no room for envy. I had come to know that any one of those things would stand between me and the healing I so desired.

My heart shall not fear.

(Psalm 27:3)

"But I'm afraid, Lord. I'm afraid You'll tell me something to do for this act of obedience that I won't be able to do."

For God hath not given us a spirit of fear.

(2 Timothy 1:7)

Nothing brings fear except unbelief. I had learned all things that stood between God and me were what the Bible calls "unclean things." I knew I had no great ability, no great education. I wasn't an orator or a minister. I felt the Lord would have someone do something great, something special, for a healing like this. I should have known He already knew my ability and wouldn't have me do something I wasn't capable of. If I'd thought that through, I wouldn't have had that fear in the first place.

"Lord, I will accept this healing for myself and now."

The Lord spoke again, "Go and say, 'God healed me,' and then testify. Go to the people who believe in healing and to the people who don't believe in healing, to the people who will laugh and to the people who will scorn."

"Oh, yes, Lord, I'll go. Yes, Lord, I'll go." That wasn't difficult at all. He called me to do something that was easy for me.

Through this one prayer God healed me.

When I said "Yes" to the Lord, He knew I meant it for yesterday, today, and forevermore. He also knew the extent to which I would go, the length of time I had and what I would do.

■ ■ ■

CHAPTER SEVENTEEN

IT WAS JESUS!

Who shall not fear thee, O LORD?
(Revelation 15:4)

The instant I said, "Yes, Lord, I'll go," Jesus gave me sight to see Him standing by my bed! I had never prayed to see Jesus. I had no idea it was even possible. I didn't see any features on my Lord's face. I saw a great light that could not be seen through and Jesus standing there in a white robe and a white mantle over His head. There was absolutely no doubt it was Jesus.

He reached over the bed rail and touched me with only the tips of His fingers and He made me whole again! I felt His warm fingers touch the area of my heart. I felt heat, like fire, in my head. It went down through my body, to my fingertips and down to the bottom of my feet. No longer was I blind, no longer was I paralyzed.

The doctor had compared my muscles to cement. When they began to break loose, I felt great pain. I heard breaking and slipping and crackling noises. I would have screamed from that pain, but the Lord was there. I was looking at Jesus! With my eyes on Him, I could withstand the pain.

I was in such awe as Jesus stood by my bed that I didn't dare say a word, nor did I dare ask one question. I just accepted what He did for me. When He touched me with the tips of

His fingers, I was made completely whole! I was never so well, before or since, as when His healing power went through my body. Oh, what joy when the Lord was there!

"I'll provide for you," He said. He wasn't just talking about bread and water and a roof. Among other things, it included removing the fear I had earlier. He told me to stay three days and three nights in the hospital, walk the halls and proclaim, "God healed me," and then testify.

"You can't go back to your old life because I'm not giving you a life to live out. I have not given you back your old life. I am loaning you this time to do this for Me."

As Jesus came to the head of my bed, He continued talking to me. Only as I raised up did I realize I was whole again. I hadn't turned over in three months, and now I was able to not only raise up, but I was whole again! I lay back down because I couldn't take my eyes off Jesus.

After Jesus left me, I saw nothing more than a light. I went into a long, deep sleep from which no one could awaken me.

■ ■ ■

CHAPTER EIGHTEEN

PRAISE GOD, LOOK WHAT HE'S DONE FOR TICER!

**This I say then, walk in the Spirit.
(Galatians 5:16)**

When I finally awoke, reluctance began creeping in. I cried, "Out there, Lord, where You told me to go, they don't know You can stand at my bedside. They don't know You can speak in an audible voice. They don't know You can come and reach out to me with warm fingers and touch me and make me whole again. When I step out there in the hall where I know people and begin to say what You told me, they'll call me a fanatic and I'll just die, Lord, I'll just die."

I didn't want to start in what was my Jerusalem, but that's where I was. I was afraid of what others might say about me. I wanted to go to some other city, somewhere else, where people didn't know me.

God had already dealt with me about that stiff-necked pride, so I wasn't reluctant for long. Realizing I was not praying, I said, "Oh, Lord, forgive me, forgive me. I'm just as guilty as the children of Israel coming out of Egypt, murmuring and complaining. Lord, if You'll forgive me, I'll never again value the opinion of man."

I can truthfully say that since that time I have not valued the opinion of men. In obeying God, man's opinion must be ignored. I cannot truthfully say I have never again slipped back into murmuring and complaining. For this I have had to ask for forgiveness. God's Word tells us how serious it is to murmur and complain before God.

Today is the day to begin doing His will. That usually means doing something simple, even saying a kind word to someone who needs it. It doesn't need to be some gigantic thing that turns the world around.

After I knew Jesus had forgiven me, I raised myself up, not really knowing how to start. From that instant, I've not been able to tell what God did for me often enough. This was in spite of the fact my church hadn't prepared me to walk out and boldly tell others what happened to me.

> This I say then, walk in the Spirit.
>
> (Galatians 5:16)

Even if a step-stool had been nearby, I wouldn't have needed it. I simply jumped over the raised bed railing and found my heavy cotton duster. Glad they hadn't thrown it away, I put it on. I put on my shoes, picked up my Bible, paused a moment, and began to walk.

Curtis, on duty, walked by. Shocked to see me up and walking, he asked, "Who came to pray?"

"Bea Schmick came to pray."

"Jonesie," a former RN on my floor, was in the bed next to me. She was paralyzed from the hips down, after being hit by a car. Since she was nearby, she knew about the funeral arrangements being made for me. When she saw me up and walking, she began screaming one loud scream after another. Because I hadn't heard any loud sounds in over three months, my eyes quickly squeezed shut at the noise. Her screams startled me as much as my walking startled her.

Curtis called out, "Jonesie, if you can't stand to see what the Lord Jesus Christ has done, I'll give you a towel to cover your eyes."

Try as I might, I could only get the tips of my toes to touch the floor. I walked not only on my tiptoes, but on the end of my toes, like a ballet dancer.

As I walked over to the door of the ward, someone asked, "Is it hard for you to walk?"

"Oh, no, it's not hard, but it's hard to get my feet flat on the floor," I replied. This was a supernatural act of God. The Lord wanted to establish this truly was a miracle that could not be made to look natural. I've since wondered what would have happened had I not tried to touch the floor at all.

As I stepped out into the hall, an orderly raised his hands and said, "Praise God, look what He's done for Ticer!"

In those first minutes, I answered one question after the other. Many who saw me first were hospital staff. Some, having known me and my physical condition before I was healed, had no doubt it was God who had done this marvelous thing.

Later, a doctor's wife placed her hands on my bed and received a jolt that knocked her backwards. After regaining her composure, she said, "Oh! That was like an electric shock!"

Long after He left, the Lord's anointing was still evident as a sign for unbelievers.

■ ■ ■

CHAPTER NINETEEN

NO SCRIPT TO FOLLOW

And they were all amazed at the mighty power of God.
(Luke 9:43)

I walked to the hospital coffee shop looking for my charge nurse, whom I loved dearly. Many there knew me. Seeing me, some passed out and some had to be helped out of the room. When I found her, I walked over and said, "Look at me. Jesus came. Jesus touched me. He made me whole again. He told me He gave me a gift of peace."

Covering her eyes with her hands, she said, "Oh, no, you can't sit! You can't stand and you can't walk! You can't get all the way down here."

"If you can't look at my face, look at one of my hands and you'll know Jesus came."

Because my hands were crippled, she had power of attorney to sign any necessary papers for me. When she brought them she'd say, "I've brought you these papers, and I'll read them to you because you have a clear mind." Or she'd say, "I'll pick up one of your hands and let it touch the pen. That might make it more legal."

She peered through her fingers to look at my hand. After lowering her hands she asked, "How many people helped you down these halls?"

"One."

"Pray tell us who."

"It was Jesus Christ Himself! It was Jesus! He helped me down the hall. Now, I'm just like you."

"How did you get out of bed with the rails up?"

"Jesus gave me the strength to jump over them!"

"Let's send for the last specialist you saw."

When the specialist arrived he just stood in the doorway looking at me and said, "A happier person I've never seen. This is surely of God."

I asked him to come in the room.

"Oh, no, Ticer, I'm as close to you as I want to be."

My hands were raised in surrender to God. I was praising God out loud. "Hallelujah! Praise the Lord! Jesus came and touched me and made me whole again!"

The words had never been in my mouth before, and no one had written me a script.

Perhaps the specialist thought my words were contagious.

Jesus came and touched me with warm fingers and made me whole again. I heard His beautiful, audible voice and knew it was Jesus speaking, and I couldn't stop praising God out loud, even in a hospital. The joy of the Lord was my strength!

The superintendent of the hospital was called. Unlike the specialist, he came and stood right next to me and said, "I don't believe in anything. You know I'm an unbeliever. I know you were an MS patient for years. I know you've been lying paralyzed and blind in this hospital. Since the Lord came and there's been a miracle here, this old hospital has rocked on its heels. Since Jesus came and there's been a miracle, there's been no work done in this part of the hospital. But, never mind the work. Look at what my Lord has done!"

Somehow, while he said those few words, he found the Lord.

I went down to the office to let them know I must leave the hospital in three days and three nights. After recovering from the shock of seeing me, the director answered, "You can't go. We must keep you thirty days for observation."

"I can't stay. Jesus told me when I was to go. If I stay even four days, I'll be out of the will of God."

■ ■ ■

CHAPTER TWENTY

DON'T JUST STAND THERE

Make a joyful noise unto the LORD.
(Psalm 66:1)

One of the required tests performed after my healing was an electrocardiogram. The doctor who did it had read the results from previous tests given every seven days since I entered the hospital. He knew the condition of my heart muscle.

He said, "I believe in healings. I know many doctors who have seen them. I turned off the machine before I was half-finished and just prayed and thanked the Lord. I've spent the major part of my career reading tapes from EKG machines. I know this is a miracle!"

On the second day, nurses came by to treat a bedsore. I asked, "Do you want to doctor me? I've never been so well in all of my life."

"It's our duty," one replied. She found no bedsore and no evidence there ever had been one, and exclaimed, "Oh, my God, my God!"

The other nurse said, "Bedsores don't go away in hours."

I said, "No, they hardly ever go away at all."

"I can't even see the bone," she said. "There's no scar, no red spot, no sign you ever had a bedsore. This is a miracle!"

> And about the eleventh hour he went out . . .
> (Matthew 20:6)

One day, I was walking down a hall, speaking and giving glory to God for my healing. Later, I was told about a man being rolled from the elevator to the door of the operating room on that floor. For some reason, the medication to put him to sleep had not yet taken effect.

He told the attendants, "That's Gertrude Ticer. I can hear her talking and I can see her walking. I talked to her when she was in a wheelchair. If God can heal her, He will heal me, too." He rose up on the stretcher, pulled the sheet around himself, walked to his room and dressed. Not bothering to get officially discharged, he left the hospital and went home.

I spoke with him two years later and asked, "How have you been since you walked out of the hospital without having your operation?"

"I haven't had the operation and I'm sure I'll never need it," he replied.

That isn't strange if you think about it. I remember the lepers in the Word who were healed as they walked away.

In Matthew 20, Jesus talks about those coming to work at 11:00 o'clock at night who received the same wages as those who came early in the morning. I didn't begrudge this man his wages because he came at 11:00 o'clock. He accepted the healing. That's what mattered.

> And straightway many were gathered together.
> (Mark 2:2)

After a Christian radio station announced a miracle had happened in the hospital, many came to see. The halls in the hospital became so crowded the workers could hardly do their work. It was like in the Book of Mark when people heard Jesus was in a certain home and they gathered in.

When I asked why people were permitted to come, someone replied, "Who's going to say they can't see what the Lord has done?" People came early in the morning. Others were still there at 2:00 A.M.

The hospital gave me a room to speak in every morning from 6:00 to 7:00 A.M. I went to bed after 2:00 in the morning and slept until 6:00 A.M. when they woke me to speak to those just getting off work. One morning, while I was waiting in the room for the people, I began singing "Just a closer walk with Thee."

Someone said, "We heard you singing. Just think, only days ago we couldn't understand what you said. You couldn't even speak then, but you can sing now, just hours later."

This miracle was not only for me. It was for those who worked in the hospital, who knew my case. They could see me walking and hear me talking in a voice loud enough now to be understood. They all saw that Jesus Christ is the same yesterday, today, and forever.

My healing is evidence of what God can do. July 4, 1962, when He performed this miracle, is no different from today to Him. Healing is for you, now, wherever you are.

I am the living bread.

(John 6:7)

The Lord told me He would take away all my desire for food to prove a person can feast on the Word of God until he or she has no desire for food. It would also prove a miracle had taken place. For months I had been on 900 calories a day and I was sure I would be hungry, but I wasn't. I only drank water and found it was no sacrifice on my part. The Lord told me He wanted people to compare this with the children of Israel in the Word who were fed manna from Heaven.

Fasting is mentioned in chapter 58 of Isaiah and the Book of Matthew. If you have things you must do, you might ask the Lord if He wants you to fast. When He has asked me to fast, He asked me to kneel, pray and feast on the Word of God during that time.

For two days I had done God's bidding. I selfishly decided to walk outside to the tree in the fenced-in area outside the hospital. Standing under the tree I said, "Lord, thank You. Thank You for healing me. I can see those leaves far up in this tree, the little leaves so beautiful, so green, so high."

As I stood there, a nurse came out and touched my shoulder. She asked me, "What are you doing out here? People are standing in the halls, waiting to see you walk."

The minute I felt her hand on my shoulder, I knew she was being her "brother's keeper." I was out of God's will. I was not doing what Jesus said to do for those three days. After I asked the Lord to forgive me, I walked back up the ramp.

Just as I stepped back into the hospital, I saw a man in a wheelchair. He raised his arms and said, "Come and talk to me."

As I walked over to him, he asked, "Are you the woman they used to tie in a wheelchair so spasms wouldn't throw her out? Are you the one who couldn't see?"

"Yes, I am."

"Oh, tell me about your Jesus. I don't know Him." This gentleman, by asking to hear about my Jesus, let me know I was where I wanted to be, back in the will of God.

After Jesus healed me, He said, "Go to Mr. Martin." When I found him in another section of the hospital, he turned his back to me.

"Please look at me, Mr. Martin."

"Go away from me. Go away."

I went back to the area I was in when Jesus spoke to me. After a while the Lord said, "Go back to Mr. Martin."

In the old days, before I had received forgiveness for false pride, I would have gone back only once. But not now. I walked back to him and asked, "Please look at me."

With his back to me again, he said, "I helped with that last spinal tap, then I had a day off. According to medical science it was impossible for you to have been here when I returned, so go away."

I walked back to the same area once more. Again, I heard Jesus say, "Go to Mr. Martin." Back I went.

"Please look at me, Mr. Martin. You know how far it is to my ward, up one hall and down another."

"I know."

"Well, just look at me."

"I'm going to. I'm a good Catholic. In my church, we don't have anything against miracles. But, it should have happened in a cathedral or at a shrine, not in a ward in a hospital."

That was what had been bothering him.

"But, Jesus can do miracles anywhere," I answered.

At that, he swung around and said, "Now, I know Jesus Christ is the same yesterday, today, and forever, and that He's still healing in a Las Vegas hospital in 1962."

He paused a moment, then began clapping his hands, shouting, "Let's do something, let's do something! Don't just stand there! Jesus has been here!"

After we walked up and down the halls, Mr. Martin urged me, "Call that woman who prayed. Bring her back to the hospital. Call your children. Let's do something!"

Jesus knew what Mr. Martin's reaction would be when he looked at me and acknowledged this miracle. He told me later, "I'm going home to Canada knowing Jesus Christ is the same yesterday, today, and forever."

■ ■ ■

CHAPTER TWENTY-ONE

YOUR MOTHER SAYS JESUS CAME

**That you may tell it to the generation following.
(Psalm 48:13)**

After I was healed the hospital called my young grandson, Tom, to come. They didn't give him an explanation so he came prepared to take my body away. When he saw me walking toward him, he collapsed and fell over a nurse's stand.

Tom finally regained consciousness and said to the nurses who were caring for him, "My grandmother was the only one who ever spoke to me about healing. She said that one day the Lord's going to make her whole." He even told the nurses about the day he asked me why I was still sitting in the wheelchair.

When he called my daughter, Martha Marshall, in Fairbanks, Alaska, to give her the news she didn't say a word, she just cried.

Randy had come earlier from California to say his last good byes to me. But when Tom called him, he didn't know the right words to use since he didn't attend church. He just said, "Your mother's well and she's walking up and down the hospital halls telling people about Jesus."

Randy answered, "I'll hang up the telephone if you say that again. The doctor has already told me about my mother."

Next he said, "Your mother says that Jesus came and touched her and He's made her whole."

"Why didn't you say that in the first place, Tom?"

When my brother, Jack, was told he said, "Praying for people and seeing them healed is one thing. But, when it's your only sister, it's an entirely different story."

When my mother heard the good news she said, "Thank You, Jesus," and asked me to come home.

■ ■ ■

CHAPTER TWENTY-TWO

GO TO NORTH LAS VEGAS TONIGHT

**For you shall go out with joy.
(Isaiah 55:12)**

When I was released from the hospital, the director said, "In spite of all the laboratory tests not yet done, in spite of all the preliminary examinations still needed, we will let you go on the exact moment your Jesus says. Even in Las Vegas, we do what Jesus says." He then said, after he shook my hand, "I have touched the hand of a person God has touched."

After I left Southern Nevada Memorial Hospital, I heard the Lord say, "Go to North Las Vegas tonight."

That afternoon a phone call had come inviting me to give my testimony that evening in a home in North Las Vegas. God was showing me I didn't need to knock on any doors.

All I had in the world to wear was my duster, a nightgown and my shoes, and I had my Bible. I had learned my lesson well about giving God excuses, not to mention pride and man's opinion. That night I gave my testimony four times in those clothes from 7:00 to 11:00 P.M. I was happy to have a pair of shoes to wear, but I would have gladly given my testimony in my bare feet. The shoes just made it better.

When I went back to the home where I would stay that night, Bea Schmick told me, "Someone from Henderson sent you some clothes." I was scheduled to speak at a church the next morning at 11:00 A.M. Bea said, "If you try on the clothes, I'll alter them while you're sleeping."

"I'm too weary," I said. "Besides, I don't believe God would send me clothes that weren't my size." The next morning when I put them on, they fit just fine.

> Rejoice and be exceeding glad.
>
> (Matthew 5:12)

I went back to see my family doctor two weeks after my release from the hospital, still walking on the tips of my toes.

"Why did you come here?" he asked.

"The doctor at the hospital asked me to."

"He only wanted me to see you since you've been healed. But I want to see the results of the sixteen hours of examination before you were dismissed. Then I want to go in the same blood vessel that was once completely dried up to see what happened, if you will allow it."

Previously, he had operated on my leg and removed ten inches of that dried-up blood vessel.

"I don't mind, if you will let me walk up and down the halls in the clinic and tell what Jesus has done for me."

"Agreed."

(I'm certain the results of what happened that day in those halls are recorded in Heaven.)

After reading my records, the doctor used a special needle to go into that blood vessel. He said, "The blood is running normally. I think the Lord made a brand new person."

"Oh, no, the Lord just remade me. He just did a good job of making me over."

"Now, tell me about the handwriting expert," he asked. "I read in your records that one was called in."

"I haven't really written anything for fifteen years, because of my crippled hands," I told him. "When the hospital's office staff checked my records, they saw a difference in my handwriting. They called in a handwriting expert to make a determination. He said my handwriting after God healed me was different from what was on record. The dismissal records would show the person they admitted was not the one they were releasing. One was not Gertrude Ticer. I asked the handwriting expert, 'What can be done? I'm still me. I'm the same person.'

"He answered, 'Get three people who saw you admitted to sign an affidavit stating you are the same person.' That's how the matter was settled. There's nothing else to say. I'm still me." ■ ■ ■

CHAPTER TWENTY-THREE

A SMALL GLIMPSE OF HEAVEN

But now they desire a better country.
(Hebrews 11:16)

When I went to my mother's, I found I wasn't home. It wasn't the same and that bothered me. I said, "Lord, I feel so misplaced. This isn't home anymore."

Because the Lord had given me a small glimpse of Heaven, nothing here on earth compares with that.

I used to like to stay home. I never wanted to travel and packing a suitcase I liked even less. But the Lord has enabled me to do both. He did say, "Go," so I try to be at home in the home I'm in. I'm very happy to do anything else He asks.

> For the testimony of Jesus is the spirit of prophecy.
> (Revelation 19:10)

My mother said she feared one day I would give my testimony and no one would believe me.

"Mother, Jesus didn't tell me to make anyone believe me. He said to go and say God healed me, and then testify. He gave it to me, I give it back. I speak to Him, not the people. I give the glory to the Lord alone.

"Those who hear may take whatever they need, whatever they wish. I just want to be sure I lift up Jesus. If people walk out, I'll keep on speaking. When I finish and see they're gone, I might be startled, but it won't bother me."

I have been asked what I think of faith healers. All I can say is, "I am not one." I have been sharing with you what the Lord has done for me, and what He told me. I lay on hands and pray because the Word says to and because Jesus spoke to me and said, "You pray and I'll do the healing." I am not the healer. Jesus is the Healer.

In the clefts of the rock . . .
(Song of Solomon 2:14)

Down in the plains of Texas they have trained dogs to chase and catch jackrabbits. Jackrabbits are smart and run fast but they can't outrun the dogs. But, turn a little cottontail loose and the dogs can't catch it. It's little and it can't run fast, but it finds a cleft in the rock and hides in that cleft.

You can anchor your soul right now to that Rock, Jesus Christ. No matter what your situation is, you can have Jesus Christ in your heart and be anchored to Him. You can hide in the cleft of that Rock.

My message to you is:

> Jesus Christ the same yesterday, today and forever.
>
> (Hebrews 13:8)

If you really believe that, you know Jesus can do anything today He did on the shores of Galilee. Though healing is a mystery to the natural man, it is no mystery to God. Jesus is the same as He was 2,000 years ago. He healed the blind and the lame. Jesus healed all who came to Him. But, some places He could do nothing because of the people's unbelief.

God never changes and He does not make mistakes. Things happened in my life I don't understand. When a loved one dies quickly, we may not understand why. That person's life may seem as perfect as any we know. It is beyond our understanding.

No matter what we seek, we must not defeat ourselves by our thoughts because God knows the very intent of our hearts. He knows how big we are, spiritually and otherwise. He also knows how big we think He is! Look to Him. If you have a need, God has a supply.

Healing is one of the dividends of the Gospel of Jesus Christ. But, healing never comes first, if things are to be ranked first, second, or third in importance. The greatest miracle is the salvation of a soul.

I can't give you any tangible proof showing how my miracle took place or explain how it happened. I know I was completely paralyzed and blind. I was nearly dead. A sheet had been pulled over me.

Then Jesus came. He touched me and He made me whole.

I have no tomorrows, this I know. I'm on His "loan time." When the Lord calls in this loan, I'll be happy to go home. The Lord has told me many things about home, where Jesus is. His time is my time, because I'm doing this for Him.

Gertrude Ticer went to be with the Lord in 1982 after crisscrossing the U.S.A. and going from Canada to South America for nearly twenty years telling others what Jesus had done for her. While paralyzed and near death, she insisted that her shoes remain by her hospital bed, ready for the day when she would walk again. After she was healed, Gertrude's feet took her wherever the Lord led her. Truly, her feet were shod with the preparation of the gospel of peace.

■ ■ ■

SOME SHORT SAYINGS OF GERTRUDE TICER

The soil of my heart hadn't been cultivated.

I had taken salvation from the Atonement but I hadn't taken healing. Healing in the Atonement is proven in Isaiah 53:5 and 1 Peter 2:24.

Once I believed in healing, I knew not how to unbelieve.

Know Hebrews 13:8. Then search the four Gospels and read about the healings of Jesus.

Can you believe God is the Master of your soul?

You can be a believer and still have unbelief in many areas.

Being made whole is different from being healed. "Make me whole" is not the same as "heal me."

Pray, don't get over in the complaint department.

Jerusalem is where you are. I wanted to leave my Jerusalem and go where people didn't know me.

I made a vow to never again value the opinion of man.

We must never defeat ourselves by our thoughts.

Please remember, I'm "sharing with" you, I'm not "telling" you.

When Jesus touched me, the warmth I felt in my head renewed my mind with the mind of Christ, removing past suffering, sorrows and pain.

There are many meanings to the Greek word "believe."

Submitting your will to circumstances is easy. Submitting your will to God is difficult.

Las Vegas may not have been ready for a miracle, but a miracle happened in Las Vegas.